AF270694

CATS

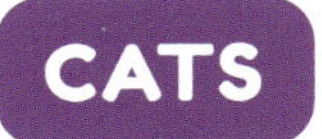

PERSIAN CATS

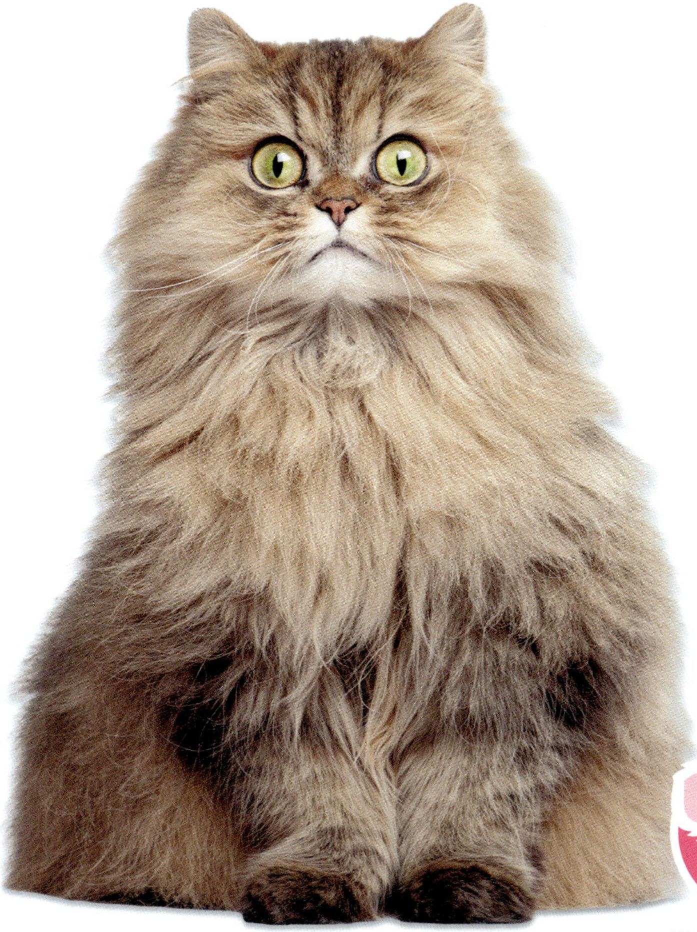

by Elizabeth Andrews

Cody Koala
An Imprint of Pop!
popbooksonline.com

Hello! My name is Cody Koala

This book is filled with videos, puzzles, games, and more! Scan the QR codes* while you read, or visit the website below to make this book pop.

popbooksonline.com/persian

*Scanning QR codes requires a web-enabled smart device with a QR code reader app and a camera.

abdobooks.com

Published by Pop!, a division of ABDO, PO Box 398166, Minneapolis, Minnesota 55439. Copyright ©2023 by Abdo Consulting Group, Inc. International copyrights reserved in all countries. No part of this book may be reproduced in any form without written permission from the publisher. Cody Koala™ is a trademark and logo of Pop!.

Printed in the United States of America, North Mankato, Minnesota.

102022
012023

THIS BOOK CONTAINS RECYCLED MATERIALS

Cover Photo: Shutterstock Images
Interior Photos: Shutterstock and Getty Images
Editor: Grace Hansen
Series Designer: Colleen McLaren

Library of Congress Control Number: 2022941111

Publisher's Cataloging-in-Publication Data
Names: Andrews, Elizabeth, author.
Title: Persian cats / by Elizabeth Andrews
Description: Minneapolis, Minnesota : Pop!, 2023 | Series: Cats | Includes online resources and index.
Identifiers: ISBN 9781098243128 (lib. bdg.) | ISBN 9781098243821 (ebook)
Subjects: LCSH: Persian cat--Juvenile literature. | Cat, Domestic--Juvenile literature. | Longhair cat--Juvenile literature. | Zoology--Juvenile literature.
Classification: DDC 636.832--dc23

Table of Contents

Chapter 1

So Fluffy

Persian cats are very fluffy. A double coat gives them their flowing mane. Their short **muzzles** and big round eyes add to their famous look.

Persian cats can have white, black, blue, cream, or red fur. They can also have different patterns.

Watch a video here!

Peke-faced Persian
Traditional Persian

The head of a Persian cat is large and round. There are many types of Persian cats. Peke-faced Persians are known for having a very flat face. Traditional Persians do not have any **extreme** features.

Chapter 2

Personality

Persian cats are gentle and calm. They are good apartment pets because they are quiet and don't climb or jump. They like to cuddle up in places like pillows, blankets, and their owner's lap.

Learn more here!

Don't let their grumpy faces fool you! Persians are sweet and loving animals. Their easy personality helps make them one of the most popular **breeds** in the world.

Persian cats prefer calm and peaceful homes.

Persian cats were one of the first breeds recognized by the **Cat Fanciers Association** (CFA). They were included in the first official cat show!

Chapter 3

Cat Care

Persians need more care than most cats. With so much fur, Persian cats must be brushed every day. They need a bath every two weeks. Their eyes should be cleaned once a day.

Explore links here!

Some Persian cats
have **kidney**, eye, or teeth
problems. Owners should
have a good veterinarian

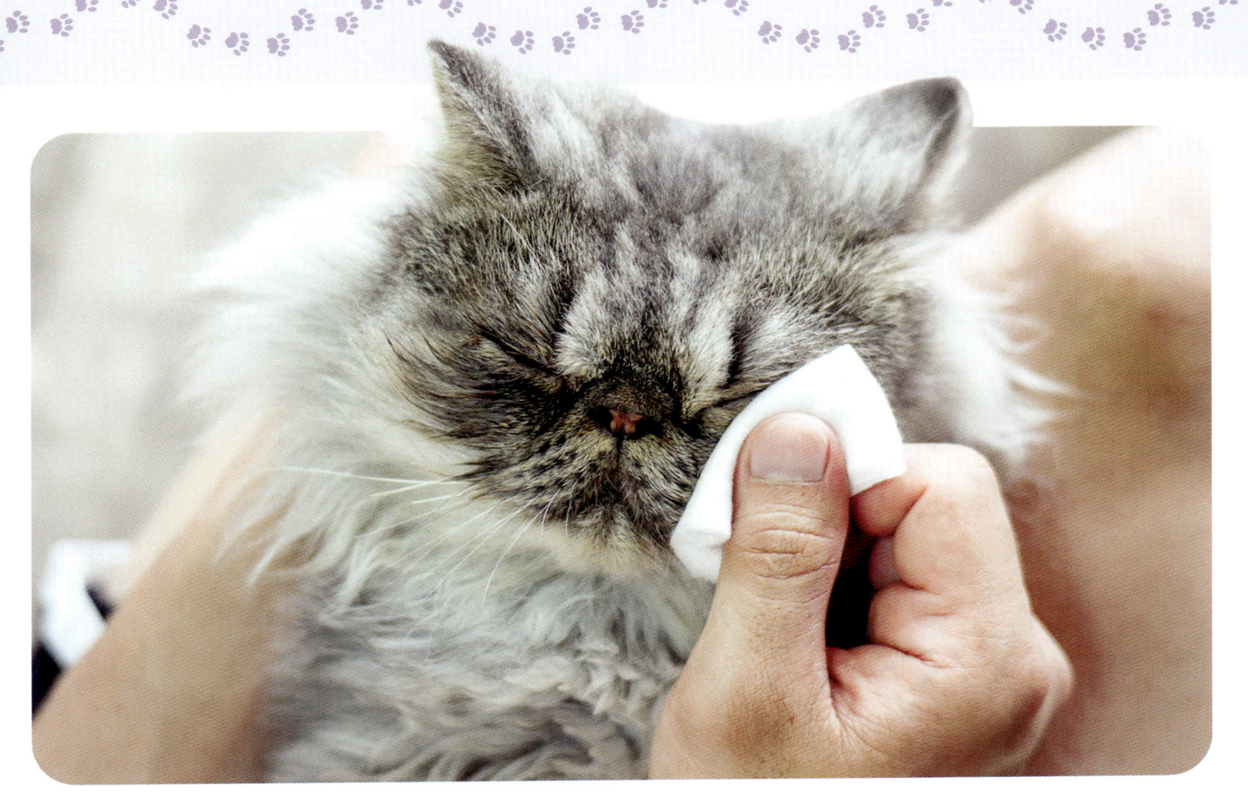

that knows the Persian cat
breed well. The cats should
visit their vet at least once a
year for a checkup.

Persian Kittens

Persian cats are born deaf and blind. They gain these senses at around three weeks old. Kittens need to stay with their mother until they are 12 to 16 weeks old.

Complete an
activity here!

It is important to start gently cuddling Persian kittens early. This helps get them ready for daily grooming. It will also help them become calm, friendly cats.

Making Connections

Text-to-Self

Do you think you could take care of a Persian cat's fur alone, or would you need help from an adult?

Text-to-Text

Have you read any other books about cats with a famous look? What did they have in common with the Persian cat?

Text-to-World

Why do you think the Persian cat is the most popular breed in the world?

Glossary

breed – a particular type or kind of animal.

Cat Fanciers Association (CFA) – a group that sets the standards for judging all breeds of cats.

extreme – of a kind that is much beyond what is average or normal.

kidney – one of a pair of organs that cleans waste from the blood.

muzzle – an animal's nose and jaws.

Index

Online Resources

popbooksonline.com

Thanks for reading this Cody Koala book!

This book is filled with videos, puzzles, games, and more! Scan the QR codes* while you read, or visit the website below to make this book pop.

popbooksonline.com/persian

*Scanning QR codes requires a web-enabled smart device with a QR code reader app and a camera.